![BBC] **DOCTOR WHO**

DOCTOR WHO
The Girl Who Died

A story based on the original script by
JAMIE MATHIESON AND STEVEN MOFFAT

Level 2

Retold by Jane Rollason

Series Editors: Andy Hopkins and Jocelyn P...

Pearson Education Limited
KAO Two
KAO Park, Harlow,
Essex, CM17 9NA, England
and Associated Companies throughout the world.

ISBN: 978-1-2922-0613-4
This edition first published by Pearson Education Ltd 2018
1 3 5 7 9 10 8 6 4 2

Worldwide

Set in 9pt/14pt Xenois Slab Pro
Printed by Neografia, Slovakia

Published by Pearson Education Limited

For a complete list of the titles available in the Pearson English Readers series, visit
www.pearsonenglishreaders.com.
Alternatively, write to your local Pearson Education office or
to Pearson English Readers Marketing Department,
Pearson Education, KAO Two, KAO Park, Harlow, Essex, CM17 9NA

Contents

In this story

The Doctor

The Doctor is a Time Lord from the planet Gallifrey, a very long way from Earth, and he is about 2,000 years old. He can fly through time and space in his time machine.

The Doctor's journeys are exciting, and often dangerous. He helps people – on Earth and on other planets – when he can. He saves people from dangerous aliens, and writes about these aliens every day in his *2,000 Year Diary*.

The Doctor never wants to kill anybody. He doesn't carry a gun, but he does use interesting technology. His sonic sunglasses can open doors and see inside things.

The TARDIS

The Doctor flies through time and space in a time machine, the TARDIS.

On the outside, the TARDIS is a blue police box from Earth. In earlier times, people called the police from these blue boxes. But the inside of the TARDIS is very different. It has a lot of technology and it is much bigger on the inside than on the outside.

The Doctor's Companion: Clara Oswald

The Doctor's companion is his friend and helper. In this story, Clara Oswald is his companion. She is from Earth, and she is an English teacher at a London school. At the end of each story, the TARDIS usually takes the companion back to Earth.

The Vikings

Vikings lived in Scandinavia – now Denmark, Norway and Sweden. From about the year 790, for 300 years, they went on long journeys across the sea. They found other places, usually in Europe, and often stayed there. They were famous for their longboats and their fighting.

Ashildr

Ashildr is a sixteen-year-old Viking girl. She lives with her father, Einarr, in a small village. She is different from other girls, and is the village storyteller. When the Doctor arrives, she is very interested in him. The Doctor is also interested in her. Is her face from the future?

The Mire

The Mire are tall, ugly aliens. They have small heads, large mouths and many teeth. They wear metal clothes, and helmets over their heads. The Mire have a lot of very good technology and they have very fast spaceships. They love war, but they aren't very good fighters. They only want to fight when they can win.

Introduction

'That wasn't a god,' said the Doctor. 'It was an alien from another planet. And those were his warriors. They took your men, and I lost my friend.'

The Doctor is talking to Viking villagers. When he and Clara arrive in a quiet wood in Scotland in the TARDIS, in the year 850, they meet some Vikings. The Vikings are not friendly. They take the Doctor and Clara with them to their home across the sea. But some aliens arrive at the Viking village at the same time, and they are looking for Viking warriors. The aliens take the best fighters – and Clara – to their spaceship.

How can the villagers fight the aliens? Will the Doctor see Clara again? And who is Ashildr? The Doctor thinks that he knows the young Viking woman – but how? This is his first time in the Viking village!

You can watch *Doctor Who* on television in Britain and in many other countries. William Hartnell played the First Doctor in 1963 – in black and white! In this story, Peter Capaldi plays the Twelfth Doctor. Jenna Coleman is Clara, his companion.

People watch *Doctor Who* on television because they love the exciting journeys to dangerous places, and the Doctor's clever tricks. Many people follow the Doctor's journeys for years and years. They start watching when they are children. Then they don't stop. Most people like one Doctor more than all the others.

You can read other stories about the Doctor and Clara in Pearson English Readers - *Robot of Sherwood, Mummy on the Orient Express, Flatline, The Woman Who Lived* and *Face the Raven*.

A Spider in Space

'Doctor!' called Clara.

'Yes, yes,' said the Doctor. 'I'll talk to you in a minute. I'm fighting Sontaran* warships!'

Clara was somewhere in space and time. The Doctor was somewhere in space and time, too. But they weren't in the *same* place in space and time.

'Doctor!' Clara called again. She looked at the strange planets all round her. 'Help me!'

The Doctor was inside the TARDIS, his spaceship. Clara was outside, in space, in an orange spacesuit and helmet. She couldn't see the Doctor, but she could talk to him through her helmet.

'Doctor!' she cried.

'I *am* busy, you know,' the Doctor answered. 'I'm in the middle of a war.'

Suddenly, there was a loud *BANG*. The Sontaran guns hit the TARDIS and the Doctor fell to the floor. The lights went off and on again.

'There's something in my spacesuit,' Clara shouted.

'I can't hear you, Clara,' said the Doctor. 'There's a lot of noise in the TARDIS.'

* Sontarans: alien warriors. The Doctor often meets them on his journeys.

'Something's moving inside my spacesuit,' she repeated. 'I can feel it.'

'Ah, yes, that's possible,' answered the Doctor. 'I think it's one of the spiders from that last planet, Metebelis 3.'

'OK,' said Clara. She tried not to be afraid. 'Tell me more.'

'Metebelis spiders live under the mountains there, and they aren't very nice,' said the Doctor. 'I think that your spider wants to eat you.'

'It's running up my leg,' said Clara. With its eight legs, the spider easily pushed its way up her spacesuit.

'You'll be fine,' said the Doctor. 'Perhaps it's hungry. Look at the planets near you. What can you see? Tell me.'

'Er ... there's a blue planet. It's quite big. There are two little yellow planets. One is bigger than the other,' said Clara. 'Doctor! It's on my back!'

'Don't think about the spider – think about the planets,' said the Doctor. 'Look between the big blue planet and the two yellow planets. Is there a green planet?'

'Yes, yes, there is,' said Clara.

A spider's leg moved in front of Clara's face, inside her helmet. It was black and hairy.

'Doctor!' she shouted. 'Please help me *now*.'

'I'm coming!' he said.

Clara fell to the floor of the TARDIS. The Doctor pulled off her helmet and the big spider fell out. He kicked it, then stood on it. It was not a nice sound.

The Doctor was a Time Lord from the planet Gallifrey. Clara was a teacher from the planet Earth. She was his companion, and they flew through time and space in the Doctor's spaceship, the TARDIS. On the outside, the TARDIS was a small, blue police box. On the inside, it was a big spaceship.

After many exciting journeys to many different planets with the Doctor, Clara never stayed afraid. She jumped up from the floor.

'Did we win?' she asked. 'Are the Philosians* safe?'

'Oh!' said the Doctor. He looked unhappy. 'Aren't you going to say thank you? The TARDIS brought you in and saved you. That's not easy, you know.'

The Doctor wasn't really unhappy. Clara knew that.

'And the Philosians?' she laughed. 'Are they safe?'

'Well,' said the Doctor, 'the Sontaran warships followed me across space and used their guns on the TARDIS. But yes, I saved the Philosians. Oh, and I also saved an English teacher. A spider wanted to eat her.'

The TARDIS made a loud noise and arrived on Earth.

'So now,' the Doctor said, 'I'm going outside. I've got a dead spider on my shoe.'

The TARDIS door opened, and Clara followed the Doctor outside. It was dark and they were in the middle of some tall trees.

'We're in the north of Scotland,' said the Doctor. 'I think the year is about 850.'

But Clara wanted to know more about the Philosians.

'Won't the Sontarans come back and fight the Philosians again?' asked Clara.

'I couldn't do any more for them, Clara,' said the Doctor. 'It says "Police" on the TARDIS, but I'm not a policeman!'

'What *can* you do, Doctor?' asked Clara. 'What *can't* you do? I never know!'

'Time Lords move through time,' he answered. 'We go to earlier times. We go to the future. We can change things in little ways. But we can't make *big* changes.'

Suddenly, they heard the sound of metal. Then they felt the cold of metal on their faces. Swords!

Big, tall men stood round them. The men wore helmets and they carried fire. They had long red hair and long swords, and they looked angry.

'Oh no,' said the Doctor. 'Not Vikings! I don't want to talk to Vikings. Not today.'

* Philosians: aliens from the planet Philosia; friends of the Doctor.

The Viking took the sunglasses off the Doctor's nose. He broke them in two and threw them to the ground.

The tallest man spoke. 'You're coming with us,' he said. He didn't smile.

'No, I'm not,' said the Doctor. 'Do you know why not? Look at these!' He took out his sonic sunglasses and put them on. 'These are from the future. You Earth people won't have technology as clever as this for many, many years.'

The Viking took the sunglasses off the Doctor's nose. He broke them in two and threw them to the ground. *Then* he smiled. The other Vikings laughed.

'Clara,' said the Doctor.

'What?' asked Clara.

'We're going with the Vikings.'

The Viking Village

The journey over the sea on the Viking ship took two long days. Clara sat next to the Doctor, and they looked across the cold water. They couldn't do anything, so they talked.

Clara asked the Doctor about his face. It was his twelfth different face. 'How do you feel about your face now?' she asked. 'When it was new, you didn't like it. Do you remember? Do you like it now? *I* like it.'

'I saw this face before it was mine,' the Doctor told her.

'When was that?' asked Clara. 'Was it before you met me?'

'Yes. I was in Pompeii*, in Italy, in Roman times. When everybody died, I could only save one man and his family. That man had this face.'

'So why do *you* have it now?' asked Clara.

'I don't know,' said the Doctor. 'But I think it will be important one day.'

Suddenly, the tallest Viking stood up in the boat.

'Mountains!' he shouted.

The other warriors stood up.

'Home!' they shouted.

---

*Pompeii: a Roman town near Mount Vesuvius. In the year 72, a river of fire from Vesuvius ran into the town. Everybody died and Pompeii disappeared.

The morning sun shone on the Viking village. Smoke came from the fires in the small wooden houses.

One villager watched the sea. Then he saw a boat – their boat! 'They're here!' he shouted.

Everybody was excited. The villagers left their work. The children laughed and ran down to the water. There was music and singing. Chickens and other animals ran everywhere.

The warriors pulled the two strangers off the boat. They pushed them across a bridge over a river and into the village.

One of the Viking villagers was a girl of about sixteen. She wore trousers, and looked different from the other girls. She walked with the warriors.

'You're safe!' she said. 'Is *everybody* safe?'

'Yes,' the tallest Viking answered. 'We're all here, Ashildr.'

Everybody was excited. The villagers left their work. The children laughed and ran down to the water.

The Doctor's mouth fell open. He watched with the villagers.

'I was afraid for you,' Ashildr told him. 'The sea is dangerous. War is dangerous. Why do you have to go?'

'We're Viking warriors,' he said. 'That is our life.'

The Viking had the Doctor's sonic sunglasses. He gave the two halves to Ashildr. She looked at them, interested.

Clara and the Doctor were a little way behind them. They walked slowly.

'Is your plan ready, Doctor?' asked Clara. 'Now is a good time for a plan.'

'Yes, I have a plan,' said the Doctor.

'OK,' said Clara. 'What is it?'

A Viking pushed the Doctor. 'Move,' he said.

They walked past Ashildr. The Doctor looked at her. She looked at the Doctor. He looked at her again.

'Who's that girl?' asked Clara. 'Do you know her?'

'No,' said the Doctor slowly. 'I never saw her before.'

'OK,' Clara said. 'So why are you looking at her in a strange way?'

'I don't know,' said the Doctor. 'It happens when you go back in time.'

'*What* happens?' asked Clara.

'You remember something from the future.'

The Doctor turned and looked back at Ashildr again. She was interested in the strange man and she stayed near them. Everybody in the village was interested in the strangers, but to Ashildr the man was more than a stranger.

'He will be important in my life in some way,' she thought. 'But how?' She looked at the sunglasses.

The Viking behind the Doctor pushed him again. 'Faster!' he said.

'OK,' said the Doctor to Clara. 'Here's the plan. We meet the chief. I do something clever. Then the villagers want me to be their new chief.'

'That's a plan?' laughed Clara. 'That's not my idea of a good plan!'

The chief waited in front of the village longhouse* in the centre of the village. He was an old man with long, white hair.

'Father,' said the tallest warrior.

'My son,' said the Viking chief. 'This is a happy day.'

'We went across many seas and mountains on our journey, Father,' said the chief's son. His name was Hasten. 'We fought hard and we fought well. We lost nobody.' Then he pushed the Doctor and Clara in front of the chief. 'And we found these two. So we brought them home.'

'Now's a good time, Doctor,' said Clara quietly.

The Doctor took a small yellow ball from his coat and threw it at the chief's helmet. It came back and he caught it.

The warriors pulled out their swords. The villagers shouted angrily. The Doctor spoke loudly to them.

'I am very angry with you,' he shouted. 'Be afraid! I have the face of a man – but I am not a man.'

The Vikings moved away.

'What *are* you?' asked Hasten.

'Don't you know me?' said the Doctor. 'I am Odin*!'

Clara started to laugh, then quickly put her hand over her mouth.

'You are not Odin,' said Hasten.

'And how do you know that?' asked the Doctor. 'Is Odin a friend of yours? Tell us about him.'

* longhouse: a large building, a home for many villagers and a place for meetings.
* Odin: the most important of the Viking gods.

'Oh, my people!' said the face. 'I am Odin!'

But suddenly, a very loud *BANG* came from the sky. Everybody looked up. There was a head in the sky – a very large head. Was it a man? Or was it a god? He wore a Viking helmet and had long black hair. He wore a strange metal square with red glass in it over one eye.

The Doctor's mouth fell open. He watched with the villagers. A yellow light shone down on the Vikings.

'Oh, my people!' said the face. '*I am Odin!*'

3

Valhalla

The Vikings fell to the ground in front of their god.

'And now, my people,' said Odin, 'listen well to my words.'

The Doctor looked at the Viking faces. To them this really was Odin.

'Don't listen to this man! He's not a god!' he shouted.

But nobody listened to the Doctor.

'I am inviting your strongest warriors to my great longhouse in the sky,' said Odin. 'They will eat and drink with me in ... Valhalla*!'

Suddenly, six metal warriors came down from the sky and appeared in the middle of the village. They were taller than the tallest Viking. They had large metal helmets with a red glass window for eyes. They carried big guns.

'What are these?' cried the old chief. 'Are these Odin's warriors? Are they our friends? Or do they want to fight us?'

The Viking warriors jumped to their feet and pulled out their swords. They stood in front of their chief and the other villagers. They wanted to fight. They were ready. But the metal warriors didn't use their guns. They looked at the Vikings carefully.

* Valhalla: the home of the Viking gods in the sky. Warriors went there when they died.

The Doctor and Clara moved out of the way of the guns. Clara looked up at the head in the sky.

'Is that really Odin?' she asked.

'No!' said the Doctor. 'Gods don't show their faces.'

'And they're not Odin's warriors?'

'No,' said the Doctor. 'They're aliens.'

'What do they want?' asked Clara. 'They're not killing people.'

'They want the strongest warriors,' said the Doctor. 'They don't want the weaker villagers or the children.'

The metal warriors began their work. They looked at each Viking through the red window in their helmet. Then they sent the chief and the strong warriors up to 'Valhalla' and pushed the weak villagers to the ground. The children were afraid.

'We have to help them,' said Clara.

'No,' said the Doctor. 'We have to stay here, on Earth.'

Somebody shouted behind Clara and she turned. A metal warrior pushed Ashildr to the ground, then moved away. Clara ran to her.

'Come back!' called the Doctor.

'Are you OK?' asked Clara. She put her arms out to Ashildr and took her hands.

Another metal warrior turned and saw them. It also saw the sonic sunglasses in Ashildr's hand. The computer inside the metal helmet was interested in the technology. The warrior moved its gun round to Clara and Ashildr.

'No!' shouted the Doctor. He started to run to them.

Before he could get there, the two women disappeared. Clara and Ashildr were on their way to Valhalla.

The metal warriors stopped moving. And then they all disappeared up into the sky.

Suddenly, it was quiet. There were no Viking warriors, no metal warriors. There was no Odin, and no Clara or Ashildr.

The Doctor looked up at the sky.

'Now what?' he thought.

Clara and Ashildr appeared on the floor of a metal room.

'Ashildr and the strange woman!' said Hasten. 'Do you like Valhalla?' He gave them a warm smile.

They didn't like Valhalla. The room was small, and there were about twenty Viking warriors inside it.

There were metal doors in one wall. Hasten pulled the doors open, and they saw a second metal room. This was larger, with two long walls. There were six round windows in each wall.

'Odin's longhouse!' said Hasten and walked inside.

'Wait!' called Clara. She put her arms across Ashildr and the other men. 'Stay back.'

But Hasten didn't listen. He stood in the middle of the second room. He opened his arms wide and laughed loudly.

'Don't be afraid, strange woman,' he said. 'Odin loves us.'

Then they all heard a different noise. The windows were not windows. They were machines and they started to turn. They turned faster. Blue and white electricity jumped out of the machines and across the room. It danced round and through Hasten. There was a *BANG*. And then the machines stopped.

The Vikings looked into the room.

'Where is Hasten?' shouted Ashildr.

'My son!' cried the old chief.

They could see a Viking helmet and sword on the floor, but Hasten wasn't there. Suddenly, the Vikings heard the sound of metal behind them.

'The wall!' shouted a warrior. 'It's moving across the floor!'

The first room was now smaller. The moving wall pushed everybody into the second room.

'Odin!' called Ashildr. 'Odin! Help us!'

The Vikings tried to push the wall back but they couldn't stop it. They were all in the second room now.

'Come with me,' shouted Clara to Ashildr. She pulled the Viking girl past the machines, to the end of the room. There were doors there too.

The machines started to turn again.

'We have to open these doors,' Clara shouted to Ashildr. 'Quickly!'

Blue and white electricity jumped out of the machines. It danced round and through Hasten. There was a *BANG*.

They put their fingers between the doors and pulled.

Now the Viking warriors were between the machines. The machines turned faster and the noise was louder. Blue electricity jumped out of the machines.

'*Agh!*' shouted the Vikings, and then it was quiet.

In the village, everybody was sad.

'They took half the village,' said Ashildr's father, Einarr.

'Yes,' said a second Viking. 'And it was the good half.'

'Our warriors wanted to go,' said Einarr. 'Who doesn't want to go to Valhalla?'

'*I* don't want to go,' said the second Viking. 'You know that I hate high places.'

The Doctor stood next to a wooden dragon with an angry face. It was for a new boat. Vikings often had a wooden dragon's head at the front of their boats.

'Valhalla!' said the Doctor. 'Do you really think they're in Valhalla? No! You're intelligent people.'

'Yes,' said Einarr. 'Be careful with your words. We *are* intelligent. We know that you are not Odin.'

'You're right,' said the Doctor. 'I'm not Odin. I'm the Doctor. And that head in the sky? You also know *that* is not Odin. How do you know?'

Nobody spoke, so the Doctor answered his question.

'Because gods never show their faces. That wasn't a god,' said the Doctor. 'It was an alien from another planet. And those were his warriors. They took your men, and I lost my friend.'

'And *I* lost my *daughter*,' said Einarr angrily.

Warrior Wine

Ashildr woke up.

'*Ssh!*' said Clara.

'Where are we?' asked Ashildr quietly.

'We're on the spaceship,' Clara said, 'but we're in a different room.'

It was a very large metal room with big, noisy machines in it. There were thick wires everywhere, and green lights went on and off.

Ashildr looked at the machines. 'What are these things?'

'I don't know,' said Clara.

'Look!' Ashildr said suddenly. 'The helmets of our warriors.'

'But no warriors,' said Clara sadly.

'So why aren't *we* dead?' Ashildr asked.

'Because of these,' somebody said from behind them.

Clara and Ashildr turned and looked at the speaker. It was 'Odin', and he had the Doctor's sonic sunglasses in his hand.

'Oh!' smiled Clara. 'Look at you! You're smaller than a Viking warrior! You're the same size as me! You're not Odin the god. You're Odin the little alien chief!'

There were two metal warriors behind him. They had their guns ready.

'What are these things?' the alien chief asked.

'Please don't be afraid,' said Clara.

'I am *not* afraid,' the alien chief said.

'But you know that those sonic sunglasses are clever technology. They're from the future, cleverer than *your* technology.' said Clara. 'And look at me. I'm wearing a spacesuit.' She turned round and showed her orange spacesuit. 'So I'm not from Earth.' Clara smiled at the alien. 'You know that you don't want to start a fight with me. You don't know anything about me. How many friends have I got? What guns have we got? Perhaps you can't win. You really don't know.'

The alien chief thought about Clara's words. She was right and he didn't like it.

Then a metal warrior walked past Clara and Ashildr with a bottle in its hands.

'What's that?' smiled Clara. She was not afraid. 'Time for your medicine?'

'Warrior wine,' said the alien chief. Now *he* smiled.

'Oh,' said Clara. 'Very nice.'

The alien chief drank quickly. Green smoke came out of his mouth.

'Mmm,' he said. 'It's as good as the finest red wine!'

'*Warrior* wine?' cried Ashildr. Her face was white. 'I don't understand. You're drinking ... our warriors? Those machines ...? They make warriors into wine?'

'*Ssh!*' Clara said to Ashildr. Then she turned back to the alien chief.

'Go! Now!' she said angrily. 'You know that you can find warriors on other planets. We won't follow you because we don't want to fight.'

'War is our way,' said the alien chief.

'But is this a *clever* war?' Clara asked. 'Or is this a *stupid* war? Perhaps you will lose it! Then what? Everybody will say, "These warriors are weak! We're not afraid of them. Let's kill them and take their spaceships. Let's take their planet!"'

The alien chief didn't answer for a minute. Then he spoke. 'Perhaps you are right,' he said. He turned to his metal warriors. 'Get ready,' he said. 'We will leave in one hour.'

But then Ashildr pushed past Clara.

'No!' she shouted. 'You killed our warriors and you will pay for that! I am Ashildr, daughter of Einarr. I am a Viking. You are not Odin. You are not a Viking! You laughed at our gods. You killed our warriors. And *we* will kill *you*!'

A wide smile appeared on the alien chief's face. 'That's better,' he said.

'No!' said Clara, and she pushed past Ashildr again. 'You're leaving. Remember?'

'Warriors do not talk,' said the alien chief.

'Yes, they do,' said Clara. 'Listen to me.'

'Warriors fight,' he answered. '*We* will fight.'

'And *we* will win,' said Ashildr.

'Please,' Clara said to Ashildr. 'You're not helping. Be quiet.'

'At ten o'clock tomorrow,' said the alien chief, 'ten of my warriors will fight the best warriors in your village.' The alien chief laughed loudly. 'Now I will send you back. Tell your people that they will all die tomorrow!'

'Why are you doing this?' asked Clara.

'Because I love war! Look into my eyes.'

He pulled off his Odin face and showed Clara and Ashildr his alien face.

'*Yeuch!*' cried Ashildr.

His face was wet and yellow, and he had dirty yellow teeth. Clara often saw strange aliens, but for Ashildr this was the first time. She felt very ill.

The Doctor walked up and down in the Viking village and looked quickly through his *2,000 Year Diary*.

Suddenly, a light shone from the sky and Clara and Ashildr appeared on the ground.

Einarr ran to his daughter and put his arms round her. 'My love!' he cried.

The Doctor ran to Clara and stopped.

'Hi,' he said, 'you're not dead.' He didn't like showing his feelings. But then he shouted happily and put his arms round her. Clara laughed. That didn't usually happen!

'Where are our men?' asked Einarr.

'I'm sorry, Father,' said Ashildr sadly. 'They're not coming back.'

'I am Ashildr, daughter of Einarr. I am a Viking. You are not Odin. You are not a Viking!'

The Doctor opened his book. 'The aliens are in here,' he said, and started to read. 'They're ...'

'Listen,' said Clara.

She wanted to tell him about the fight, but he didn't listen.

'... the Mire.'

'Listen!' Clara tried again.

'The Mire are dangerous warriors but they aren't stupid,' read the Doctor. 'They don't fight wars when they don't have to. Good. Now, tell me that they're leaving, Clara. They listened to you, right?'

'*How* dangerous?' asked Clara.

'What?' asked the Doctor.

'You said, "They're dangerous". *How* dangerous are they?' asked Clara.

'They're *very* dangerous,' the Doctor said. 'Why?'

'Because I think that this village is at war with them.'

5

The Viking Way

In the longhouse, Clara and Ashildr told the villagers about the Mire and their spaceship.

'They're coming here tomorrow,' Clara said. 'Ten of them. They want to kill everybody in the village.'

'Ashildr, is this right?' asked Einarr.

'Yes,' Ashildr answered, 'and it's because of me. I didn't listen to Clara. I wanted to fight – and now they are going to kill all of us.'

'It wasn't Valhalla,' said another man sadly.

'No,' said Ashildr. 'And it wasn't Odin. The alien chief pulled off his Odin face. We saw his Mire face. I was afraid and then I was angry. He laughed at us and our gods. And I started a war with him.'

There was a fire in the middle of the room. The villagers sat and looked at it. Mothers put their arms round their children. The old people talked about earlier, happier days. The young people talked about the future. There *was* no future for their village.

The Doctor walked up and down. *He* didn't look sad.

'Smile!' the Doctor told the villagers. 'Yes, the Mire are coming. That's bad. But not for twenty-four hours! And that's good. You can run a long way in twenty-four hours. Leave the village. Don't come back for a week.

The Mire will come. They'll see a village with nobody in it. There won't be a fight. They'll leave Earth and go back to their spaceship!'

Einarr stood up. 'We can't leave this village,' he said.

'Yes, you *can* leave!' said the Doctor. 'Climb into your beautiful boats with their wooden dragons and go across the sea. Or swim across the river and run through the trees up into the mountains. It's easy.'

'No!' Einarr said. 'That is not the Viking way. We will stay and fight.'

The Vikings stood up. 'We will fight!' they shouted.

'Really?' said the Doctor. 'Perhaps you don't remember? They took your fighters. And you, here, what can you do? You can cook and catch fish. You can look after animals and use computers ... Oh no, you can't do that. But can you *fight*? Do you have *swords*?'

'Every Viking has a sword!' said Einarr.

The Doctor was angry now. 'OK, let's see. Who in this room can fight with a sword? Put your hands up.'

Only two people put their hands up – the Doctor and Clara.

'The Mire are coming,' the Doctor said. 'What are you going to do? Are you going to throw vegetables at them?'

'*I* can throw vegetables,' said the cook.

'I think the stranger is being funny,' said the Viking next to him.

'We are Vikings,' repeated Einarr. 'We do not run and we are not afraid of dying. We will fight for our village and we will die for our village. That is the Viking way!'

'Yes!' said the villagers.

Nobody spoke for a minute. Then a baby started to cry.

'Will your *babies* die for the village?' asked the Doctor. 'Are babies afraid of dying?'

Everybody listened to the baby's cries. The Doctor closed his eyes.

'The baby is saying, "I am afraid",' he said.

'He, er, speaks "baby",' Clara told the villagers.

'"Mother! Mother, you are beautiful. I will sing for you. I am afraid but I will sing",' the Doctor said.

Nobody moved. They listened to the baby's words and felt sad. Then the baby was quiet.

'I understand the Viking way,' said the Doctor. 'In the future, the world will remember you. You're strong people. You're strong, but you're stupid too. I'll be sad when you all die.'

He walked to the door of the longhouse. Ashildr followed him.

'Please stay,' she said. 'You can help us. I know you can. And we will listen to you.'

'You want my help?' answered the Doctor. 'Then, run!'

He looked at Ashildr and then back at the other villagers. He went outside.

Clara followed him. She knew the Doctor. He wanted to save them but he didn't have a plan.

'The planet is safe,' he said. 'This is one small village.'

'One small village?' smiled Clara. 'You don't mean that. *Every* small village is important to you.'

'OK,' said the Doctor, 'let's think about it. Perhaps we *can* save the village. And remember, we have no TARDIS, no sonic sunglasses, so it will be very, very difficult. But, OK, we save the village. The Vikings win and the Mire lose. Wonderful! But then what's going to happen? Suddenly, everybody on other planets is going to talk about Earth and plan a visit. More Mire will come. They'll want some of this famous Viking warrior wine. Think about it. We can save twenty lives in a small fight, but a bigger fight will follow the small fight. Then there will be a war. And in the end, everybody will die.'

The baby started to cry again. They listened.

'What's it saying?' asked Clara.

'*She*, not *it*,' said the Doctor. 'She's afraid. Babies feel dangerous times. "Mother, I hear noise in the sky. I hear shouting. You are my world, but I hear other worlds now. I'm afraid. You are kind, but will the other worlds be kind? The sky is crying now. Fire and water ..."' He closed his eyes. '"Fire and water,"' he repeated slowly. Those words were important. But why?

Clara knew that face. She smiled warmly. 'You're having an idea,' she said. 'So we're staying!' She walked back to the longhouse. At the door, she turned to him. Chickens ran round her feet. 'The baby isn't crying now,' she said.

6

Fire in the Water

'Right!' said the Doctor, with a sword in his hand. The strongest Viking men stood in front of the longhouse. 'When I say "Move," you move. When I say "Jump," you jump.'

One of the Vikings put up his hand.

'Yes, what is it, Lofty?' asked the Doctor.

'Er ... my name's not Lofty,' said the Viking.

'I can't learn your names – I haven't got time,' said the Doctor. 'I'm going to give you names. Then I'm going to teach you fighting. So you're Lofty.' He named the second man Daphne. The third was Noggin and the fourth was Heidi. 'Oh, and Limpy,' said the Doctor. Limpy was the cook.

Clara and Ashildr watched. First, the men fought with wooden swords.

'How can we fight those metal aliens?' asked Ashildr. 'We are not strong warriors.'

'The Doctor is thinking of a plan,' answered Clara. 'When it's ready, it will be a *good* plan.'

'Now,' shouted the Doctor, 'let's try a fight with metal swords.'

'Yes!' shouted the Vikings.

'Now,' shouted the Doctor, 'let's try a fight with metal swords.'

The fight with metal swords didn't go well. First, Einarr hit Noggin on the head with his sword. Noggin fell to the ground and his helmet flew off. His helmet hit a horse. The horse kicked Limpy. Limpy fell into the fire. Wood from the fire flew into a house. And then the house was on fire. Everybody shouted and ran for water. They threw water over Limpy and the fire.

The Doctor and Clara sat outside the longhouse. The Doctor had his head in his hands.

BANG! BANG! Clara looked up at the dark sky.

'What's that?' she asked.

'It's the Mire,' said the Doctor. 'They're making Mire guns. They want us to hear them.'

'Well?' asked Clara. 'We've got about twenty hours. What's your plan?'

'*This* is my plan,' said the Doctor. 'The Vikings have to fight.'

'But you don't *like* fighting,' said Clara. 'And they'll never win a war with the Mire.'

'Vikings are happy when they die well.'

'Is that your best plan?' cried Clara. 'They can die well?'

'Only gods never die,' said the Doctor. 'People can't live for all time.'

Ashildr came out of the longhouse and walked past them. She looked back at the Doctor.

'Did you hear that?' asked the Doctor.

'Yes, sorry,' she said.

'No,' said the Doctor. '*I'm* sorry.'

'Goodnight, Ashildr,' said Clara.

Ashildr said goodnight to Clara but looked at the Doctor.

'She likes you,' said Clara.

'Stop it,' said the Doctor. 'I'm an alien.'

'*I* like you,' said Clara. 'I love my life with you.'

'Clara,' the Doctor said slowly. 'I have to say something.'

'No,' said Clara. She knew his next words before he said them. 'You do this every time.'

'Everybody will die tomorrow,' he said. 'But *you* don't have to die. Will you please leave?'

'Don't ask me that,' she said.

'These people died many, many years before you were born, Clara,' said the Doctor.

'I'm not going to run away,' she said angrily. 'You know that I never run away.'

'You're here because I brought you here,' he said.

'No!' answered Clara. 'I'm here because I *want* to be here!'

'OK, think about this,' said the Doctor. 'The Mire will come tomorrow. They'll kill everybody. They'll kill *you*. What then? How do I live with that?'

'Don't think about me,' said Clara. 'Think about the village. Stop playing with swords. Start to look for the answer. How can the Vikings win? How can *you* win? There's always an answer and you always find it. So look for it!'

She stood up and went back into the longhouse. The Doctor looked up at the dark blue sky and the planets. Clara was right. There was always an answer.

'But what *is* the answer?' he thought. 'How *can* I win? I have no idea.'

At the end of the village, near the river, was Ashildr's little house. She lived there with her father. After she said goodnight to the Doctor and Clara, she went back there. She lit a fire. Light from the fire danced round the room. Einarr stayed in the longhouse with the villagers.

Ashildr was very unhappy about the fight with the Mire. Because of her, there was no future for the village or for anybody in it. She wanted to cry.

In the middle of the room was a wooden man. She put a Viking helmet on its head and gave it a wooden gun. Now it was the Mire chief. In the light from the fire, it looked bigger than it was.

'"Odin"! We meet again!' she said. She walked round the wooden man with her wooden sword. 'Valhalla is on fire! Your metal men are dead!'

The Doctor came into the room, but Ashildr didn't see him.

'Now, "Odin",' she shouted, 'you are going to die!'

She hit the wooden man hard with her sword.

'Ah,' said the Doctor. 'Ashildr, the storyteller.'

'Oh,' she said, and turned quickly. 'When did you come in?'

The Doctor didn't answer but looked at her wooden Odin.

'I love theatre and storytelling,' he said. 'It can teach us a lot.'

'I tell stories when I am afraid,' said Ashildr. 'When the warriors go out, I tell stories about their journeys.'

'You want them to be safe,' said the Doctor. 'And stories help.'

'Why are you here?' asked Ashildr.

'I'm looking for a plan, an idea,' answered the Doctor. 'Can we win tomorrow, do you think?'

'At this time tomorrow,' said Ashildr sadly, 'we will all be dead.'

'Why don't *you* run?' asked the Doctor. 'There's a big world out there. You're young. You can live your life.'

'This is my place,' answered Ashildr. 'My sky, my mountains, my river, my sea, my people. Where is *your* place?'

'I enjoy looking at beautiful places too,' said the Doctor.

'But ...?' Ashildr asked.

'But I want to see *new* places. I don't want to see the same place every day.'

'I feel sorry for you,' said Ashildr.

'And *I'll* be sorry when you all die,' said the Doctor.

'Do you think the villagers are stupid?' asked Ashildr.

'Yes, they *are* stupid,' said the Doctor.

'But they are also kind and strong,' said Ashildr. 'And I love them.'

'Good. But that won't save you.'

'I am different and strange, I know that.' said Ashildr. 'When I was little, the girls all asked me, "Are you a boy?" The boys all said, "You're a girl." There are many stories in my head. But here, they love me. They are kind to me. You tell me that I can run. You tell me that I can save my life. I tell you that I cannot leave this place.'

Ashildr's father came into the house. He was sad, and he put his arms round his daughter.

'I can't save you,' he said. 'I can't save the village.'

Then they heard the baby through the window. Lofty walked past the house with the baby in his arms.

'Where's he taking her?' asked the Doctor.

'To the boathouse,' said Ashildr. 'When she can't sleep, the baby likes the fish.'

The Doctor suddenly remembered the baby's words. '"Fire and water",' he repeated quietly. Those words were important. 'No! That's wrong. The baby didn't say "fire *and* water". She said "fire *in the* water".'

He ran out of Ashildr's house and down to the boathouse.

'Clara! Clara!' he shouted. 'I've got a plan! Follow me!'

Lofty and the baby were in the boathouse. There were many big wooden barrels in there. Lofty and the baby looked into one of them, and the baby laughed.

The Doctor ran in and looked in the barrels. He smiled at Lofty.

'Lofty!' he called. 'You're a dad! She's your baby. I didn't know that.'

Clara arrived, with Einarr and Ashildr. 'OK,' she said. 'You're shouting. What happened?'

'Nobody is going to bed tonight,' said the Doctor. 'We've got a lot of work.'

'What are we going to do, Doctor?'

'There's going to be a war tomorrow,' the Doctor answered. 'And listen to this: We're going to win!'

'How?' asked Clara.

The Doctor showed her one of the barrels. Suddenly, electric blue light shone from the water inside it. He ran to the next barrel. More electric blue light!

'Because this village has eels! Electric eels!' shouted the Doctor. 'Why did nobody tell me? Look!' he said. 'Fire in the water!'

The Fight

The longhouse was noisy that night. The Doctor gave everybody a job and the villagers worked hard. They brought metal to the longhouse – from their kitchens and from the boathouse. They brought wood to the longhouse – from their gardens and the boathouse.

The longhouse was a large building with high windows. It had one and a half floors: a big room below and stairs up to a half-floor above. People could watch the village meetings from up there.

Lofty and Einarr carried four wooden barrels from the boathouse up the stairs. The village also had one large metal bath. They pulled that up the stairs too. Noggin and Heidi brought water from the river. Ashildr brought the electric eels. Other Vikings cut open Clara's spacesuit. Inside the spacesuit were many metres of metal wire. They pulled it all out.

Clara showed Limpy her phone.

'It's easy,' she said. 'We're going to put pictures on this. Watch me. I'm starting to film ... now! OK? Can you do that?'

'I can do that,' said Limpy.

The villagers worked hard and the Doctor told them about the plan.

'We have to get one of their helmets,' he said. 'That's the most important thing. When we have a Mire helmet, they're dead.'

Morning came, and sunlight shone in through the windows of the longhouse.

'When the Mire get here, look happy,' said the Doctor. 'Never look afraid. Always walk fast and talk loudly. Be strong.'

They waited. The time came. The Mire chief and ten Mire warriors arrived, ready for war. They appeared in the centre of the village with their guns.

They looked round. The sun shone and the birds sang. But where were the Vikings?

'They are afraid!' said the Mire chief. 'They know that they are going to die!'

The chief and his warriors walked to the longhouse and pushed open the great doors. Inside, they found the Vikings.

'Ah, here they are,' he said.

The Mire chief and ten Mire warriors arrived, ready for war.

But they didn't find Vikings with swords. They found a Viking party with music and games! Men and women danced. The children and old people watched from the back of the longhouse.

The Doctor and Clara danced to the chief.

'Hello!' called the Doctor. 'Come in! I'm the Doctor. You met Clara yesterday.'

'It is time for fighting,' said the Mire chief.

Behind him, Lofty moved slowly and carefully. Four metal wires came down from the floor above. He quietly put the end of the first wire into the back of a Mire helmet.

'No, no, no!' the Doctor said to the Mire chief. 'We don't want a war. We like *parties*! And this party is for you and your lovely metal friends!'

Lofty put the end of the second wire into a second Mire helmet.

'Listen to me, Vikings!' shouted the Mire chief. 'You fight or you die.'

Lofty moved to a third Mire helmet.

'We have no guns,' said the Doctor, 'and there are no swords in this room. The computers in your helmets will tell you that.'

Lofty now put the fourth wire into a fourth Mire helmet. This time, the Mire warrior felt Lofty's hand. It turned with its gun.

Everybody stopped dancing. The music stopped.

'*Now!*' shouted the Doctor.

Up on the floor above, Einarr pushed the metal wires into a barrel of electric eels. Blue electricity jumped across the longhouse. It ran everywhere. The four Mire warriors with Lofty's wires on their helmets disappeared in a ball of electric light.

'Four down,' shouted the Doctor. 'Six more.'

The Mire chief shouted angrily at his six warriors, 'Kill them!' The Mire turned to the villagers. They ran.

'*Again*!' shouted the Doctor.

Einarr was next to the village bath. This time, he pushed wires into a different barrel. The electricity from the eels ran through the wires to the metal bath. The electricity made the bath into a very strong magnet. A helmet flew from a Mire head and up to the magnet. Then a gun flew out of a Mire hand and up to the magnet too.

'*Yeuch!*' cried the villagers, when they saw the Mire without its helmet. Ashildr was right! The Mire were very, very ugly, with a lot of dirty yellow teeth in a dirty yellow face. The children were afraid. 'Don't look,' the old people told them.

But the Doctor wasn't interested in Mire faces. He wanted the helmet.

'*Ready!*' he shouted up to Einarr.

Einarr pulled the wires out of the water. The electric light disappeared and the helmet fell back to the floor. The gun fell too, and Clara caught it.

She turned to a Mire warrior. 'Don't move,' she shouted.

The fight began. The Mire guns were loud and there was shouting. Most of the villagers ran out of the open doors of the longhouse and pushed the doors shut from the outside. The Mire warriors turned to the doors, and the only light in the longhouse now was from their guns.

At the back of the longhouse, the Doctor worked quickly on the wires inside the Mire helmet.

'How's it going?' asked Clara.

'I think it's working,' he said. Then he called Ashildr.

Noggin and Einarr carried the Viking chief's big wooden chair into the middle of the longhouse.

Ashildr sat in the Viking chief's chair. She looked very small. The Doctor put the heavy Mire helmet on her head.

'Are you ready?' he asked.

'I am afraid,' she said.

'You were born for this,' said the Doctor kindly. 'Show them your story. They will never forget it!' She saw his smile through the red window of the helmet. Then she started to think, hard. Now she was Ashildr, the storyteller. She told the story of a Viking dragon. And the Mire saw her story in their helmets.

Suddenly, the doors to the longhouse opened.

'I can't see ...' shouted the Mire chief. 'The sunlight ...'

Out of the sunlight came a dragon. It was taller than ten Mire. The Mire chief and his warriors moved back through the longhouse, away

Out of the sunlight came a dragon. It was taller than ten Mire.

from the dragon. They were very afraid.

'Kill it!' shouted the Mire chief.

But the dragon laughed at their guns. Its large head came into the longhouse; fire and smoke came out of its mouth.

'What is this ... dragon?' shouted the Mire chief. 'It is not possible! This planet does not have dragons!'

'To the spaceship!' shouted the Mire warriors. 'To the spaceship!'

'No!' shouted their chief. 'Stand and fight!'

'Are you running away?' laughed Lofty. 'Is that the Mire way?'

The Mire warriors flew up to their spaceship.

'Come back!' shouted the chief angrily.

But they didn't come back.

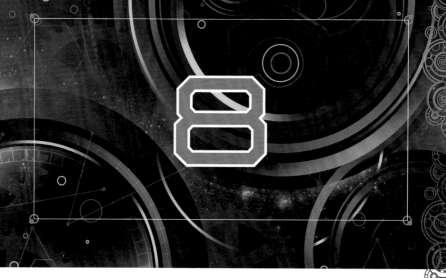

The Girl Who Died

'You can stop now, Ashildr,' called the Doctor. 'That's the end of the story. And it had a happy ending!'

The Mire chief watched the dragon through his red glass. It wasn't really a dragon. It was wooden, only the size of a man, from the front of a Viking ship.

The Viking villagers stood with their swords round the Mire chief. They smiled; he did not smile. He looked very stupid.

'What game are you playing?' he asked angrily.

'You're playing games too,' said the Doctor, 'with your Odin face in the sky! When you play with technology, technology can play with you too.'

Behind the Doctor, Clara spoke quietly to Limpy. 'Did you film it?' she asked.

'Yes,' he said, and put Clara's phone in her hand.

'Great!' she said.

'You Mire, you look at the world through technology,' the Doctor said. 'Sometimes that's a mistake. The stories say that the Mire warriors are the most dangerous in space. We know now that the stories are wrong. Today, you lost to a village with no warriors. These Vikings catch fish. They cook lunch. They have babies. But your famous warriors were afraid of them! The big metal Mire ran away from a wooden dragon, back to their spaceship!'

Everybody laughed.

'That was really funny,' said Clara.

'Why didn't we film it?' the Doctor said to Clara. 'Oh, wait a minute, Limpy *did* film it!'

Clara played the video on her phone. It showed the Mire warriors. In the film, they ran away from the wooden dragon.

'Leave Earth now and go back to your spaceship,' the Doctor said.

'We will meet again,' said the Mire chief. 'This is not the end of the story. I will not forget and you will pay. You will pay with your life!'

'And then what will I do with our little film?' asked the Doctor.

'Leave Earth now and go back to your spaceship,' the Doctor said.

'Everybody out there on other planets will love it! They'll see the wooden dragon and the Mire warriors and they'll laugh. "Are these the famous Mire warriors?" they'll say.'

The Mire chief said nothing.

'What's more important to you? One Time Lord in the year 850? Or the name of the Mire warriors for all time?'

The Mire chief had the two halves of the Doctor's sonic sunglasses on his helmet. The Doctor took them back. He put them on and the Mire chief disappeared.

The Vikings ran outside and looked up. The Mire spaceship left the sky above their village.

Everybody shouted and laughed. But not everybody was there.

'Ashildr!' called Einarr.

They all ran back into the longhouse. She was in the Viking chief's chair with the Mire helmet on her head.

'You did it!' her father said. 'Ashildr! You saved us!'

She didn't answer and she didn't move.

'Take the helmet off her,' said Clara. '*Now!*'

Lofty and Limpy took the heavy helmet off and Ashildr fell to the floor. Einarr caught her in his arms. Clara took her hand and looked at the Doctor.

'I think ... Doctor!' Clara said sadly. 'Ashildr's dead!'

'I'm sorry,' said the Doctor. 'I'm really very sorry.'

He ran outside.

Clara found the Doctor in the boathouse. He looked at his face in a barrel of water.

'The helmet killed her,' Clara said.

'*I* killed her,' said the Doctor. 'I used her. I hate losing ...'

'You *didn't* lose,' said Clara. 'You won.'

'I didn't mean the war,' the Doctor said. 'I don't hate losing *wars*. I hate losing *people*. I didn't want to lose Ashildr.' He turned unhappily to Clara. 'Look at you and your big eyes,' he said. 'You're strong and kind. One day, I'll lose *you*. When that happens, I'll get in my blue box. I'll run from planet to planet. But it won't help. When I arrive in a new place, I'll always see your face.'

'She died but you saved the village,' said Clara. 'What more could you do?'

'Time Lords *can* change things,' said the Doctor. 'But usually we don't want to. I told you. We don't want to change things in a *big* way.'

He looked at his face in the water again. Suddenly he understood something.

'Oh!' he said. 'My face.'

'What is it?' asked Clara. 'What's wrong with your face?'

'I saved that man in Pompeii,' he said. 'Remember? I told you about it on the boat.'

'Yes, in Roman times. That man had your face,' Clara said.

'And now that face is telling me something.'

'What?' Clara asked.

'It's telling me that I save people. I'm the Doctor and I save people.' Then he looked up at the sky. 'Are you listening?' he shouted to the sky. 'I'm going to save her.'

9

The Doctor's Mistake

Ashildr was on a bed in the middle of the longhouse. Her father and Clara were next to her and the Vikings sat round them. Her eyes were shut. She didn't move.

The Doctor was working fast on the Mire helmet.

'What is he doing?' asked Einarr.

'He's saving Ashildr, I think,' said Clara.

There was a lot of technology in the helmet. The Doctor looked at it carefully with his sonic sunglasses.

'Ah! Here it is,' he said. He showed them a small white square in his hand. 'Mire medicine. I'm changing it so it works for Vikings.' He put the white square on Ashildr's face, above her eyes. Everybody watched. Nobody said anything. Slowly, the white square disappeared.

'Where is it?' asked Einarr.

'It's inside her,' the Doctor said. 'She'll never be ill again.' Then he spoke to her. 'Ashildr,' he said, 'wake up. This isn't the end of the story.'

'Daughter,' said Einarr, 'listen to me. Come back to us. We lost our best warriors. We lost our chief and our chief's son. We cannot lose you too. Please.'

Everybody waited.

And then Ashildr opened her eyes.

Everybody started to talk at the same time. Einarr put his arms round his daughter.

'She'll feel better in a day,' said the Doctor. 'She'll be on her feet in three days. No sword fighting for a week.' He smiled at Clara. 'Now, Lofty, do you have a boat for us? Can you take us back across the sea to the TARDIS?'

Lofty and Noggin went to the boathouse.

'Let's go, Clara.'

'Wait!' said Einarr. 'Ashildr will want to see you before you go.'

'She'll see me often in the future,' said the Doctor.

'What do you mean?' asked Einarr.

The Doctor didn't answer, but he gave something to Einarr. It was a second small white square of Mire medicine.

'Do I put this on her head?' asked Einarr.

'No, it's not for her.'

'Who is it for?' asked Einarr.

'She can give it to somebody, in the future,' said the Doctor.

Before Einarr could ask more, Ashildr spoke. 'Doctor, thank you,' she said weakly.

'Don't thank me today, Ashildr,' said the Doctor. 'Don't thank me today.'

After two days on the sea, the Viking boat arrived back in Scotland. Lofty left Clara and the Doctor near the TARDIS, and said thank you for their help. The Doctor and Clara walked through the trees to the blue police box.

'You didn't say a word on the boat,' said Clara. 'What's wrong? What are you thinking about?'

'Ashildr and the Mire medicine,' said the Doctor. He opened the door to the TARDIS. 'It won't stop working. She can never get ill.'

'Well ... good!' Clara said.

'No,' said the Doctor. 'She can never get ill ... and she can never die.'

'So why did you give her *two*?' Clara asked.

'She can live for all time,' the Doctor answered. 'But that's not good because other people die. Your family, your friends ... you live and they die. In the future, she'll fall in love with somebody. The second Mire medicine is for that person.'

The Doctor and Clara were inside the TARDIS.

'I'll take you back to Earth,' he said. And the TARDIS started to make its strange sound. Usually the Doctor liked to be funny on their journeys. But not this time. He could only think about Ashildr and her future.

'Was it a mistake?' he asked. 'I make mistakes sometimes. Ashildr isn't a Viking now. I changed her. There's some alien inside her. She's half-Viking, half-Mire. Will she be happy? Or will she hate me?'

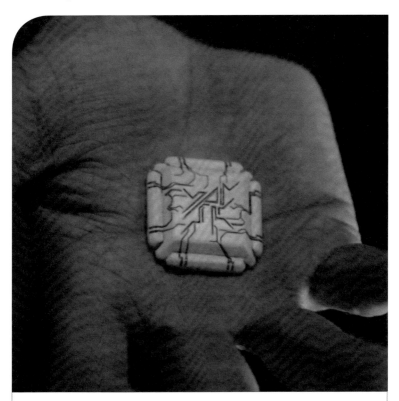

The Doctor didn't answer, but he gave something to Einarr. It was a second small white square of Mire medicine.

'Was it a mistake?' he asked. 'I make mistakes sometimes. Ashildr isn't a Viking now.'

Ashildr lived through many days and nights and years. She didn't get ill and she stayed the same age. She lived happily in her village, with her father and her friends. But one after the other they all died. She made new friends, but they all got old too. Then *they* died. Did she have to stay young for all time? Did she have to *live* for all time? Her smile disappeared.

Activities

Chapter 1

Before you read

1   What do you know about **Doctor Who**? Do you watch it on TV? What does the picture on the front of the book tell you about it?

2   Look at the Word List at the back of the book. Answer the questions.

   a Which are words for animals?
   b What can you wear on your head?
   c Which is a word for Xbox, Google and computers?
   d What can you use in a fight?

3   Read In this story on pages iv - v. Who or what:

   a teaches English?
   b can see inside things?
   c takes the Doctor and his companion through time and space?
   d tells stories to other villagers?
   e wears metal?
   f doesn't like killing people?

4   Read the Introduction on page 1 and answer these questions.

   a When does the story happen?
   b Where do the Vikings take the Doctor and Clara?
   c Who take the best Viking warriors?
   d Why will Ashildr be important in the story?

While you read

5   <u>Underline</u> the best words in *italics*.

   a When the story begins, Clara *is / isn't* in the TARDIS with the Doctor.
   b There's a *Sontaran / spider from Metebelis 3* inside Clara's spacesuit.
   c The *Sontarans / spiders from Metebelis 3* are using their guns on the TARDIS.

d The Doctor *isn't interested in / asks Clara about* the planets round her.

e The Doctor *saves / doesn't save* Clara.

f He *also saves / can't save* the Philosians.

g The TARDIS brings the Doctor and Clara to *the planet of the Sontarans / a Scottish wood*.

h Vikings with *swords / guns* take the Doctor and Clara away from the TARDIS.

i The tallest Viking *is / isn't* afraid of the Doctor's sonic sunglasses.

After you read

6 Discuss these questions with other students.

a Where will the Vikings take the Doctor and Clara? What will happen there?

b Are the Doctor and Clara good friends? How do you know?

Chapters 2-4

Before you read

7 The Doctor and Clara want to get back to the TARDIS. The Doctor is going to think of a plan. What will it be, do you think?

While you read

8 Write the words in the sentences.

a The Doctor remembers his .... from Pompeii in the year 72.

b The Vikings see the .... Then they know that they are home.

c Ashildr is always .... when the warriors are away from home.

d When the Doctor sees Ashildr, he remembers something from the ....

e Clara doesn't think the Doctor's plan is ....
f The Vikings .... think that the Doctor is Odin.

9 Which of these sentences are right (✓).

a Odin invites the Doctor to his longhouse in the sky.
b The metal warriors take the strongest Viking warriors.
c The Doctor wants to go with the Vikings to the spaceship.
d The aliens take Ashildr and Clara because Ashildr has the Doctor's sonic sunglasses in her hand.
e Hasten thinks that they are in Valhalla.

10 Answer these questions. Write Yes or No.

a Is Clara afraid of the aliens? .....
b Is the alien chief interested in the sonic sunglasses? .....
c Does the alien chief drink the Viking warriors? .....
d Does Clara want to fight? .....
e Does the alien chief want to fight? .....
f Does Ashildr want to fight? .....
g Is the Doctor happy when he sees Clara? .....
h Are the aliens leaving without a fight? .....

After you read

11 Discuss these questions.

a Why is Hasten happy on the spaceship?
b The aliens nearly leave Earth. Why don't they?

Chapters 5-6

Before you read

12 Ashildr and Clara are in the village again. What will they say about:

a Valhalla and Odin?
b the warriors?
c ten o'clock the next day?

While you read

13 <u>Underline</u> the wrong word(s). Write the right word.

    a The Mire are coming because of Clara. ....

    b The young people talk about happier times. ....

    c A baby starts to laugh. ....

    d The baby can't hear the Mire. ....

14 Who or what:

    a is going to teach fighting? ....

    b kicked Limpy? ....

    c are making guns? ....

    d doesn't want to run away? ....

    e does Ashildr hit with her wood sword? ....

    f hears Ashildr's story? ....,

    g is carrying the baby in the boathouse? ....

    h has a plan? ....

After you read

15 Work with two other students. You are all from the Viking village. Talk about Ashildr. What is different about her? How do you feel about her?

Chapters 7-9

Before you read

16 Think about these questions.

    a Chapter 7 is 'The Fight'. Who will fight? Who will win?

    b Chapter 8 is 'The Girl Who Died'. Who is the girl? How will she die?

    c Chapter 9 is 'The Doctor's Mistake'. What mistake will the Doctor make?

While you read

17 Which of these happen? Tick (✓) the boxes.

    a Clara teaches Limpy to film on her phone.

    b The Mire find the Vikings in their boats on the sea.

    c Lofty puts wires into the backs of all ten Mire helmets.

d The fourth Mire warrior feels Lofty's hand.
e Four Mire disappear in a ball of fire.
f Einarr makes a strong magnet with the use of electricity.
g The Doctor puts a Mire helmet on Ashildr.
h Ashildr tells a story in her head and the Vikings see it inside their helmets.
i A wooden dragon comes into the longhouse.
j The Mire think the wooden dragon is a real dragon.

18 **Finish these sentences.**

a Limpy .... the Mire warriors.
b Everybody on other planets will .... when the Doctor shows the film.
c The Doctor takes his .... from the Mire chief's helmet.
d When Einarr takes the Mire helmet off Ashildr, she is ....
e The Doctor didn't want to .... Ashildr.
f He never wants to lose ....
g The Doctor is going to .... Ashildr.

19 <u>Underline</u> the best words in *italics.*

a The Doctor is working on a *Mire / Viking* helmet.
b He uses his *2,000 Year Diary / sonic sunglasses.*
c The white square from the helmet is *medicine / a magnet.*
d The Doctor and Clara go across the *sea / mountains* to the TARDIS.
e The Doctor *thinks / doesn't think* that Ashildr will see him again.
f Ashildr can give the second square of medicine to *her father / somebody in the future.*
g Ashildr *can never die / will die one day*.

After you read

20 What different things do the Vikings use in their fight with the Mire? Write them down.

21 Ashildr will never die because the Doctor gave her Mire medicine. Was that a mistake, do you think? Why?

Writing

22 You are the Doctor. You want to write about the Viking story in your **2,000 Year Diary**. You will want to remember the story when you meet the Mire again! What happened? What did you learn about the Mire? Write notes.

23 You work for a TV show. Today, Ashildr is going to appear on the show. Remember, she was born before the year 850. What questions will you ask her? What do you think she will say? Write six questions and Ashildr's answers.

24 Look at the photos in the book. Write about one of them. Who is in the photo? Where are they? What is happening? What happened before this? What will happen next?

25 Think of new aliens for a **Doctor Who** story. Write answers to these questions: What planet do they come from? Are they clever or stupid? Are they ugly or beautiful? Are they angry or friendly? What language do they speak? What do they fly in?

26 You are the Doctor's companion. The Doctor asks you, 'Where do you want to go?' Think of a time and a place. Why do you want to go there? Write your conversation with the Doctor.

27 You are Lofty. The Doctor and Clara took you in the TARDIS to London for a day, in our time. Now you are back in the Viking village. You tell the villagers about your visit. What was different there? What was the same? What was **really** strange? Did you like it? Write your words.

28 You are a Mire warrior. You are going to talk to your chief's boss about planet Earth. Make notes in answer to these questions; then write fifty words. Who did you see on Earth? Where and how do they live? What happened to you there? (Don't tell the boss about the dragon!)

29 Read about one of these in books or on the Internet. Then write about it. Find pictures and put them on the page too. *Pompeii electric eels   the Vikings*

Word List

alien (n) When the strange *alien* spaceship flew over London, everybody was very afraid.

appear (v) After a man in black *appeared* in front of our house for the sixth time, we called the police. The man *disappeared* when he heard the police car.

barrel (n) In earlier times, ships carried food and wine across the sea in large *barrels*.

chief (n) The *chief* is the most important person in the village.

dragon (n) The *dragon* flew down from the mountain and over the sea. Fire came from its mouth.

electric (adj) I turned on the *electric* fire because I was cold. It doesn't work without *electricity*. *Electric eels* are river fish. They live in rivers and make electricity.

god (n) Thor was one of many Viking *gods*. Now you can see stories about him at the cinema.

helmet (n) I always wear a *helmet* when I'm on my bicycle.

machine (n) You can make ice-cream in a *machine* or by hand.

magnet (n) The boy lost some money in the tall flowers, but he found it with a *magnet*.

medicine (n) When the girl forgot her *medicine*, she felt very ill.

metal (n/adj) I cleaned the *metal* cup and it shone beautifully.

planet (n) The spaceship left Earth and flew to the nearest *planet*.

save (v) The dog jumped into the river and *saved* a little girl from the dangerous water. I never feel *safe* in the sea.

space (n) You can't walk in *space* without a *spacesuit*.

spider (n) All *spiders* have eight legs and most have eight eyes.

sword (n) Before guns, people fought wars with *swords*.

technology (n) Sarah loves *technology* and always has the newest iPhone.

war (n) The Vikings fought many *wars* in Europe. Everybody was afraid of Viking *warriors*.

wire (n) The *wire* broke and the picture fell to the floor.